Bridging the Gap

Steve Miller

Learning Media

Contents

1. From One Side to the Other

You *have a problem. You and your friends want to ride your bikes in an empty lot, but there is a small stream in your way. You don't want to get wet feet, so what can you do? How about putting a cardboard carton across the gap? You know that won't be strong enough to hold you. A fallen tree trunk won't bend, but how are you going to move such a heavy tree? In the corner, there is a long wooden plank. With a rock under each end, it's perfect for crossing the stream. Congratulations! You have just designed and made a bridge.*

People build bridges where they need to cross water, **ravines** and valleys, rail tracks, or other roadways. Some bridges, like the Golden Gate Bridge in San Francisco, are very famous.

The Golden Gate Bridge is over a mile long and has a main **span** that stretches 4,200 feet. It joins the city of San Francisco with the Marin Peninsula.

Many of the bridges you might cross when you take a trip are smaller. Some are so small that you might not even notice them. Bridges over small streams and ditches don't look very important, but without them, you couldn't drive very far. Next time you take a long drive, try to count all of the bridges you cross. You might be surprised how many there are.

In this book, we'll explore the three main kinds of bridges – beam, arch, and suspension – and there'll be a challenge for our team of young engineers at the end of each section.

Fact File

- The city of Venice in Italy has over a thousand bridges. They are needed to cross the many miles of canals in the city.

8

- Many European bridges built hundreds of years ago do more than just cross a river. They also have small stores where walkers can shop as they cross.

- Sometimes it takes a long time to make a bridge. Japanese engineers worked for 20 years designing the Akashi-Kaikyo Bridge before they started to build it.

2. Beams across the Gap

A plank of wood across a stream is the simplest kind of bridge – a beam bridge. The banks on each side of the stream hold up the ends of the beam. This was the first kind of bridge ever made. Maybe someone cut down a large tree so that it fell across a gap.

Modern beam bridges are made of metal and concrete.

single-beam bridge

If it's too long, even the strongest beam will begin to sag. But bridge builders *can* join a lot of short beams together with **piers**. The ends of the beams rest on the piers, in the same way as they rest on the banks of a river.

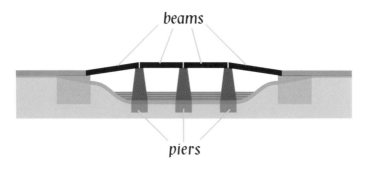

beams

piers

This old beam bridge has flat stones joining the piers.

You can make a beam bridge stronger by using a **truss**. Most trusses have triangle shapes in them. Triangles are strong shapes, so they make the beam a lot stronger. Trusses can be above the beam, below the beam, or sometimes even above *and* below.

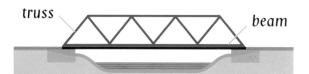

truss   beam

Fact File

- The world's longest beam bridge is in Hotseh, China. Its beams stretch from pier to pier for 90 miles.

- The oldest known bridge that is still standing is the Sweet Track Bridge in England. It was built about 3800 B.C.

- The bridge that crosses the Firth of Forth in Scotland is supported by iron tubes 12 feet thick. The total weight of the bridge is more than 56,000 tons.

Bridge Challenge

TASK: Build a beam bridge, with a truss, strong enough to hold a model train.

MATERIALS: Popsicle sticks, card, glue

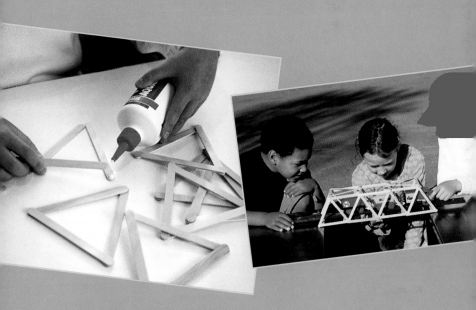

RESULT: We tried the beam on its own, but it wasn't strong enough. Then we made the triangles and then glued them to the beam. It was strong enough to hold the train.

3. Strong Arches

An arch is also a very strong shape. It is often used in bridges that carry heavy weights.

Arch bridges can be built to be very high above water so that boats can pass under them easily.

The **deck** of an arch bridge can be on top of the arch, or it can hang from **cables** below the arch. Some arch bridges even have decks that go right through the middle of the arch.

deck

arch

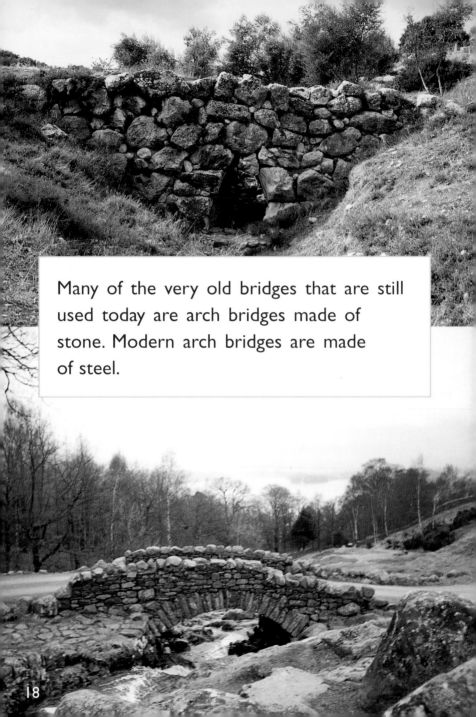

Many of the very old bridges that are still used today are arch bridges made of stone. Modern arch bridges are made of steel.

The New River Bridge in West Virginia is almost 1,800 feet long, stretching over a river canyon. A single-beam bridge would not be strong enough to cross this wide gap, and the canyon is too deep to use piers.

Fact File

- The oldest known stone arch bridge is the Nimrod Bridge in Iraq, built about 1800 B.C.

- The strength of the Sydney Harbour Bridge in Australia was shown by putting 72 locomotives on it – a total weight of 15,000,000 pounds.

- Some arch bridges and **aqueducts** built over 2,000 years ago are still being used today.

- The New River Bridge in West Virginia is the highest steel arch bridge in the world – over 1,000 feet above the canyon floor. People actually jump off this bridge with parachutes.

Bridge Challenge

TASK: Build an arch bridge across a two-foot gap, strong enough to hold a model truck.

MATERIALS: Card, glue, tape

RESULT: The card on its own would hold hardly any weight. It sagged in the middle. With the arch underneath it, the bridge was a lot stronger. It could hold the weight of the truck.

4. Hanging from the Sky

Some of the world's most famous bridges are suspension bridges. They often look as if they are hanging from the sky. A beam or an arch can only cross a gap of about 2,000 feet without using piers, and it's a big job to build piers in deep water or very deep valleys. Suspension bridges need only two **support towers**, usually on land or in the shallow waters near the shore.

main cable

support tower

stringers

deck

anchor point

The main cables hang between the two towers. The ends of the cables are attached to strong **anchor points** on land. Smaller cables, called stringers, hang down and hold the deck in place.

Early suspension bridges didn't look so amazing. They were made of rope and wood and must have been very wobbly.

Small suspension bridges today have a wooden or steel-mesh floor hanging on two cables. These bridges sway back and forth so much that they're sometimes called "swing bridges."

Have you ever wondered how people get the cables into place on a suspension bridge? Early bridge builders came up with a plan. They tied a long string to an arrow. An archer shot the arrow across the gap. They used that string to pull over the big rope to build the bridge. Today there is an easier way to start the cable. Tugboats or helicopters are used to take the first cables across.

Fact File

- The oldest suspension bridge still being used is the An-Lan Bridge in China, built about 960 A.D.

- The main span of the Akashi-Kaikyo Bridge in Japan is nearly 6,000 feet long. When the bridge was almost finished, an earthquake moved the ground underneath the towers. Now the support towers are almost six feet further apart than they were on the plans.

- The main cables of a suspension bridge are made of lots of smaller cables, about as thick as a pencil, all twisted together. If all the small cables in the Verrazano Narrows Bridge in New York were stretched out end to end, they would travel around the world more than five times!

Bridge Challenge

TASK: Build a suspension bridge to cross a
three-foot gap, strong enough to hold a
toy truck.

MATERIALS: Drinking straws, string,
glue, card

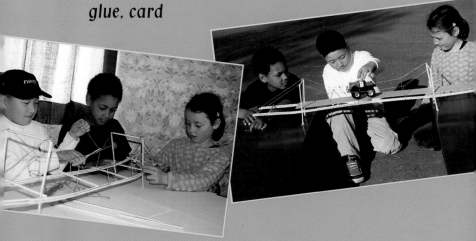

RESULT: We built the deck of the bridge first
and then the towers. The cables and the
stringers were the hard part. It took a long
time to get them just right. Our bridge
looked a bit wobbly, but it was strong
enough to hold the truck.

5. Beautiful Bridges

Whether they are designing beam, arch, or suspension bridges, engineers want their bridges to be strong and safe. They also want them to be different from each other – interesting to look at and fitting in well with their surroundings. Look at all of these designs. Are they beam, arch, or suspension bridges?

Glossary

(These words are printed in bold type the first time they appear in the book.)

anchor point: a way of holding something heavy in place

aqueduct: a special kind of bridge that carries water across a river or valley

cable: a very strong rope made from metal wire

deck: the roadway of a bridge

pier: a support that a beam bridge rests on

ravine: a steep, narrow valley

span: the distance between the two supports or piers of a bridge

support towers: tall towers that hold the cables of a suspension bridge

truss: a way of using triangle shapes to make a beam bridge stronger

Index